MASON MAKES MONEY!

Candace Okin

MASON MAKES MONEY. Copyright 2020 by Candace Okin. All rights reserved. No part of this publication may be reproduced, distributed, or transmitted in any form or by any means, including photocopying, recording, or other electronic or mechanical methods, without the prior written permission of the publisher, except in the case of brief quotations embodied in critical reviews and certain other noncommercial uses permitted by copyright law.

For permission requests, write to the publisher, addressed "Attention: Permissions Coordinator," 205 N. Michigan Avenue, Suite #810, Chicago, IL 60601. 13th & Joan books may be purchased for educational, business or sales promotional use. For information, please email the Sales Department at sales@13thandjoan.com.

Printed in the U. S. A.

First Printing, August 2020

Library of Congress Cataloging-in-Publication Data has been applied for.

ISBN: 978-1-953156-08-2

"What do you want to be when you grow up?" Ms. Robinson asks.

I sit down at my desk with a sigh.

My name is Mason, and since starting the second grade, it seems like everything is harder.

I slide down in my seat clutching my lucky green eraser, hoping Ms. Robinson won't call on me.

"Firefighter!" I hear Jaden yell from the back row.

"Engineer!" someone else says.

I don't know what I want to be when I grow up. Who can concentrate on things that far in the future? Especially when such troubling things are happening RIGHT NOW!

Like what just happened on the playground to my friend Kendra. It's bad enough that she doesn't have many friends, and that kids in class pick on her sometimes. But at recess, I saw some third graders push her off the swing and laugh at her while pointing at her shoes.

"Your shoes have holes!" I heard them saying before running off.

My mom taught me not to ever make fun of other people. It was something she said when I volunteered with her at the *homeless shelter*. So I knew just what to do.

I ran over and helped pick Kendra up off the ground. "Are you okay?" I asked her. She nodded and quickly wiped her eyes.

"I like your shoes," I said with a smile. "If you want, I can push you on the swing. As long as I'm here, they won't bother you." Kendra smiled and got back on.

When it was time to go back to class, we walked inside together, and although Kendra looked happy again, what those bullies did continued to bother me.

When we get back to class, Ms. Robinson passes back our science tests, and I see a big red B at the top, even though I studied really hard to make an A. And NOW I'm expected to know what I want to be when I grow up.

I'm relieved when I hear other classmates continuing to give answers. "Astronaut!" Eli chimes in.

"Anyone else?" Ms. Robinson asks. The classroom goes silent.

Ms. Robinson looks to the left. "How about you, Kendra?" Kendra looks up at our teacher.

I turn to her and smile, hoping that she is still feeling better, but her face turns sad again, like it did outside on the playground with those bullies. She stays silent for a while.

"Kendra?" Ms. Robinson says again.

"I don't know what I want to be. I just want a safe place for my mom and me to live."

Ms. Robinson looks concerned. "What do you mean?"

Kendra looks down at her hands. "Right now, we live in a shelter because we don't have a place of our own. I just want my own bed in my own room. That's all."

My heart sinks down through my stomach and into my shoes. I don't have everything I want, I think to myself, but I do have a warm bed with my favorite airplane sheets my mom let me pick out.

I try to imagine having to sleep in the bunks I saw at the homeless shelter. I didn't want to think about my friend Kendra being there. I have to help her again. But how?

I think about Kendra all through math, all through lunch, and all through spelling.

When I get home, I sit on my front porch, put my face in my hand, and think. There has to be something I can do, like the way Mom helps homeless people by feeding them.

Arf, arf.

I look up to see my neighbor, Ms. Guillory, and her cocker spaniel, Frankie, who runs over to me and licks my face. I play with her almost every afternoon. I throw a tennis ball for her, and she brings it back to me.

I look at the ball, still thinking about Kendra. My thoughts go back and forth like me, Frankie and the tennis ball.

My mom raises money for the people at the shelter. Could I raise money for Kendra?

Kendra doesn't need food, though. And places to live like apartments and houses must cost a lot of money.

Could I really help her? I don't even know what I want to be when I grow up, how can I find a way to get money now?

Arf! Frankie nudges me to throw the ball again.

I raise my arm and throw the ball. Frankie runs off for it.

"Maybe I can't raise money like Mom, but I can make money myself to buy Kendra her own room!" I say with excitement.

After all, that's how my parents provide for me; they make money. That's it, I'll get a job!

After dinner, I ask my parents what I can do to make money.

"Like when you're grown up?" Dad asks.

"No, now."

"What do you need money for, Mason? What about your allowance that you get for doing well in school and for doing your chores?" Mom says.

"It's not enough. I want to help my friend Kendra have her own room. She lives at a shelter." My parents look at me with surprise.

"I'm very proud of you for wanting to help someone in need," Dad says, stacking our empty plates.

"But where do I start?" I take the last drink of my milk. "Do I start by getting a job? And where do I go to get one?" I carry my glass to the sink. "Can I work with you, Dad?"

"You'll have to make money on your own; you're too young for a job, job, Mason," Dad says as he washes the dishes.

Mom turns and wipes her hands on a towel. "First, grab a pencil and some paper. You need *goals* and a plan to accomplish your goals."

I unzip my backpack and look for what I need. My parents both sit at the table.

"Let's write it all down. Then you will know how you may need to make your money, and how much you need to save."

"Save?" I ask. What did she mean by save? "Can I just work, get the money, and then buy whatever I want?"

"Yes," Dad says, "but you must keep what you *earn* and let it *accumulate* to make sure you will have enough for what you want to buy."

My mind starts spinning. How do grownups do this?

"You see, you must also take into account your *expenses*. You need to pay your expenses and still have enough to buy what you want."

"How do I do that?"

"We'll create a *budget* to help you." "Where will I save the money?" I ask.

"Adults usually save their money in a bank account, but we can save your money here at home where you can count it and keep track whenever you need to," Dad responds.

Jobs. Savings. Budgets. I feel very grown up learning all these new things. There's so much more to making money than I had known.

Tucked in tight with my airplane sheets, I can't sleep. I keep imagining different jobs I can do to earn money.

I can have a lemonade stand, but I'd have to buy the ingredients and cups first.

My big cousin Sam makes money by cutting grass, but I'm too small to push the lawnmower.

What about delivering newspapers, like my dad said he did when he was young? But I still can't ride my bike that well. I touch the scab on my right knee that I got last week when I fell off my bike.

I head out for the bus stop the next morning, still thinking about the jobs that I can do. None of my ideas seem right.

Ms. Guillory walks onto her porch and waves. Frankie runs out from behind her and sits at her feet. Her butter-colored coat looks extra shiny today; she must have just gotten a bath.

Hmmmm…

I like dogs. Maybe I can bathe Ms. Guillory's dog for her. And when I get really good at it, she can mention me to her friends, and I can bathe their dogs. Then I would really be in business!

When I get home from school, I tell Dad about my idea.

"That's a great idea, Mason. You'll need a webpage so that people can know about what you do. They can even sign up and pay for your services. I will build one for you."

Wow! My very own webpage! Dad pulls out his laptop. "One important question, son. What will you call your business?"

"Mason's Wash and Wag," I blurt out. I don't know where that name came from, but I like it anyway. Dad works on my webpage, and in no time it is done.

"Now that we know what your business is, let's set some more goals," Mom says. "How much money do you want to save for Kendra?"

"A THOUSAND dollars." I gulp. That seems like the biggest number in the world. Ms. Robinson taught us to count to one thousand once, and it took forever!

"Okay, kiddo. That's a big goal, so let's break it into smaller goals."

We figure out that I can charge $25 per dog wash and do ten dog washes a month to reach my goal in four months.

The next morning, I ask Ms. Guillory if I can bathe Frankie on Saturday.

"Of course, Mason. How much will it cost?" I puff out my chest to feel brave. "$25."

She smiles and reaches in her purse to pull out one 20-dollar bill and one 5-dollar bill and hands them to me.

"Thank you, Ms. Guillory. I'll see you at 10am on Saturday. And if you like my service, can you tell your friends about me? I have a website and everything!"

"I certainly will," she says.

One Saturday afternoon, Eli and Jaden walk by my house. I have three dogs lined up for grooming.

"Why are you washing all those dogs?" Eli asks.

"I have a job so I can make money."

Jaden's eyes get big as saucers. "You mean you get paid to wash dogs?"

I nod. The black German shepherd shakes her wet coat, covering all three of us with water.

"Can we get paid to help you?" Eli asks.

I think for a moment.

Right now, I can wash three dogs on a Saturday, but two more of Ms. Guillory's friends wanted me to wash their dogs today.

I had to tell them no because I didn't have time.

If I have two more helpers, then we can wash nine dogs in the time it took for me to wash three by myself.

"I'd love for you two to help me. Let me ask my parents first how that can work for my business."

That night, Mom helps me keep track of my *income* and expenses through the budget.

It helps me to see how much money came in, how much went out, and how much money I've saved so far. Then, we double-check the budget by counting the money in my Mason jars.

"Mom," I say in between tens and fives. "I want to hire Eli and Jaden so we can wash more dogs. How much should I pay them?"

"Okay. When you pay them, that becomes part of your expenses, just like the shampoo and brushes."

We figure out that for each dog wash, I can pay them $10.

That still helps me get to my goal faster.

Now, instead of making $75 a week, I can make $165 with Eli and Jaden working for me.

I *hire* Eli and Jaden to wash the dogs with me, and they're excited to help and make money.

We wash poodles, labradoodles, shit-zus, and even a saint bernard.

Eli, Jaden, and I work on the weekends and on school days after we finish our homework, and each day after we're done, I hand them the money they earned.

After another month goes by, I sit down with my mom to count all the money I've made and to review my budget.

We add in all my profit from having my friends working with me and subtract the expense of paying them.

I look at the number at the bottom of the column in shock.

$1,000.

Although my budget said it would take me 4 months to reach my goal, it only took 3 months to save a thousand dollars!

"I'm so proud of you!" Mom says. "Now that you've saved this money, how do you want to give it to Kendra?"

"Let's tell Ms. Robinson!"

The next day, Mom walks me into class. I hold an envelope with all the money I saved in it.

"Ms. Robinson, I have a gift for Kendra. I started a dog washing business and saved a thousand dollars for her."

"Wow!" Ms. Robinson says. "How did you think to do such a kind thing?"

"My dad helped me with the website, my mom helped me with the budget, and Eli and Jaden worked with me to wash the dogs."

"Mason, this will make Kendra and her mom very happy. Since her mother lost her job, they've gone through some hard times."

Soon, Kendra's mom walks her into the classroom, and Ms. Robinson brings her over to us.

"Mason is a very special friend to Kendra who wants to give you something," Ms. Robinson said.

Kendra moves behind her mother and looks at me with curiosity.

"I wanted to help Kendra, so I decided to save a thousand dollars so she can have her own room." I hold out the envelope to her. Kendra looks at her mom, then back at me. She looks happier than I've ever seen her.

I thought her mother would smile, too, but instead, she starts to cry.

I look up at Mom confused. "Why is she sad?"

Mom has tears in her eyes, too. "She's not sad, Mason, she's very happy, and we're all very proud of you."

Even Ms. Robinson wipes tears from her eyes.

Kendra's mother leans down to face me. "Thank you. According to my budget, this is the exact amount we need to secure an apartment. And thanks to you, Mason, Kendra will have her own room very soon."

After kids at my school learned how I saved money, they started asking me lots of questions about it:

"Can you teach me how to save money?" "How did you start a business?" "How do you make money?"

Ms. Robinson helped me to organize and *market* my business, and soon, kids from my class and other classes start to skip recess to come to me to learn how to make money.

My business is still going, but it's even bigger today.

I no longer wash dogs myself. Instead, I pay other kids to do it.

I don't need Mom to look over my budget because I do it myself.

Now I know what I want to be when I grow up. I want to have lots of knowledge about making money so that I can help others make money, too.

GLOSSARY

Accumulate

When something accumulates, it gets bigger and larger in size. If you let money accumulate, you will continue to have more money.

Budget

A budget is a document which shows all of the money you make and the money you must spend. Creating a budget will allow you to see the money you have, your expenses, and what is left over afterwards.

Earn

To earn money is to receive it for something that you do. If you do chores around the house and your mom pays you $10, you have earned that money.

Expenses

An expense is the money that you spend on something. For instance, your parents pay a rent or a mortgage expense for the place where you live.

Goal

A goal is something that you want to accomplish. What are your goals? Do you want to become a scientist or fly a rocket to the moon? Do you want to be the best soccer player on your team, or make an A on your next spelling test? Use the goals sheet to write your goals and plan how to achieve them!

Hire

When you hire someone, you agree to pay them for doing a job for you.

Homeless Shelter

A homeless shelter is where people go who do not have a place to live. Homeless shelters provide a bed where people can sleep until they are able to find their own place. Over half a million people in America are homeless,[1] and 150 million people across the world are homeless.[2]

Income

Income is the money you receive regularly. When you work, you get a paycheck. Your paycheck is a source of income.

---

1 https://www.whitehouse.gov/wp-content/uploads/2019/09/The-State-of-Homelessness-in-America.pdf

2 https://yaleglobal.yale.edu/content/cities-grow-so-do-numbers-homeless

Market

To market something means you're promoting it and letting everyone know about it. When you're selling something, you want to tell as many people as possible so that many people will buy it.

My First Budget

Let's learn how to balance and create a budget just like Mason! Fill out this worksheet step by step to learn how setting a budget can help you reach your goals.

Step 1: Savings Goals

List your top 3 goals (things you wish to do or have). Next, write down the cost and how much you hope to save each month. Then you'll need to write down how many months it'll take to reach your goal, based on your savings per month.

Description	Cost	Savings per month	# Months
	Total $ Goal		

Step 2: Weekly Income

Add up your weekly income below.

Allowance	
Earnings	
Gifts	
Other	
Total Income	

Step 3: Expenses

Add up your weekly expenses below.

Description	Amount
Total Expenses	

Step 4: Weekly Savings

Determine your weekly savings by subtracting your total expenses from your total income.

Total income   −   Total Expenses   =   Weekly Savings

My Goal Sheet

The best way to reach your goal like Mason is to plant the seed of your idea and plan it out! Use this sheet to help you achieve your goal!

Plant the seed!

My goal is _____

I want to reach this goal because _____

Date I started my Goal _____

I must reach my goal by _____

Next Step

Actions to reach my step
-
-
-

First Step

Actions to reach my step
-
-

Next Step

Actions to reach my step
-
-

I achieved my goal on this date. _____

MEET CANDACE OKIN

CHILDREN'S AUTHOR & ENTREPRENEUR

Driven by a mission to encourage reading and writing in children, Candace Okin creates literary works that aim to ignite curiosity, creativity and excitement through the reading process. A Dallas native, she's since planted roots in Houston, after which she earned a degree in Broadcast Journalism from Texas Southern University, and a Masters in Psychology degree from Houston Baptist University. Since then, Okin has crafted an impressive background in communication, marketing strategies and more.

Inspired by a desire to engage children through imaginative literature, Okin uses her work to highlight practical life skills against the backdrop of the strength and immensity of Black History and culture. Her goal is to educate youth while encouraging a sense of wonder, self-worth and purpose through the limitlessness of the arts, history and language.

Her first offering, Mason Makes Money, chronicles a child's journey through fundamental concepts of entrepreneurship and money management in a fun and engaging story as told by Mason; a thoughtful and resourceful second-grader who is eager to help a friend in need.

Alongside writing, Okin enjoys traveling, reading, and spending time with her husband Mark, son Mason, and extended family and friends. Readers can connect with her through any of the following channels:

Website: www.candaceokin.com
FB: www.facebook.com/CandaceOkinBooks
Twitter: @CandaceOkin
IG: @Candace.Okin

www.ingramcontent.com/pod-product-compliance
Lightning Source LLC
Chambersburg PA
CBHW061114070526
44583CB00027B/3291